Learning Languages:

A Fast and easy guide for beginners to learn any foreign language

Table of Contents

Introduction

Chapter 1: Get into the mindset

Chapter 2: Break down the language

Chapter 3: Immerse Yourself

Chapter 4: Usage

Conclusion

© Copyright 2017 by Mastermind Self Development- All rights reserved.

The follow eBook is reproduced below with the goal of providing information that is as accurate and reliable as possible. Regardless, purchasing this eBook can be seen as consent to the fact that both the publisher and the author of this book are in no way experts on the topics discussed within and that any recommendations or suggestions that are made herein are for entertainment purposes only. Professionals should be consulted as needed prior to undertaking any of the action endorsed herein.

This declaration is deemed fair and valid by both the American Bar Association and the Committee of Publishers Association and is legally binding throughout the United States.

Furthermore, the transmission, duplication or reproduction of any of the following work including specific information will be considered an illegal act irrespective of if it is done electronically or in print. This extends to creating a secondary or tertiary copy of the work or a recorded copy and is only allowed with express written consent from the Publisher. All additional right reserved.

The information in the following pages is broadly considered to be a truthful and accurate account of facts and as such any inattention, use or misuse of the information in question by the reader will render any resulting actions solely under their purview. There are no scenarios in which the publisher or the original author of this work can be in any fashion deemed liable for any hardship or damages that may befall them after undertaking information described herein.

Additionally, the information in the following pages is intended only for informational purposes and should thus be thought of as universal. As befitting its nature, it is presented without assurance regarding its prolonged validity or interim quality. Trademarks that are mentioned are done without written consent and can in no way be considered an endorsement from the trademark holder.

Introduction

Congratulations on downloading Learning Languages: A Fast and easy guide for beginners to learn any foreign language and thank you for doing so.

The following chapters will discuss the best way for you to learn a brand new language - any language that you'd like to, in fact.

This whole book is based off of a technique that I've developed in quite a while of studying language. I've found that it's the method which works best with my brain in particular. The method is based around breaking down language learning into small easy to learn chunks, *understanding* the core concepts underlying each and every language that you work with, as well as emphasizing the concept of immersion.

I have a huge number of qualms with conventional language learning techniques. For a long time, the typical manner used to learn another language was to simply start from the very beginning.

Language learning is like learning anything else, and frankly, if you're trying to teach a child mathematics, you don't teach them subtraction one week and then long division the very next, because long division builds off of other concepts that you've already worked with before.

However, as a result of the information age, the language learning paradigm has dramatically shifted. It started with somewhat of a shift back in the 1990s when early forms of language learning software began to hit the market. And, certainly, one could always go to the local bookstore and pick up this or that book, and even get engrossed in various methods such as the *Pimsleur* method. If they wanted to be immersed, their options were either moving to the country of the language they wanted to learn, special ordering books (and VHS tapes after a while), or watching Spanish television if they were learning Spanish in particular.

In other words, linguistics became a rather exclusive club. Today, you can just Google "how to speak Korean" or "how to speak Danish" and go from there. Even 20 years ago, though, that was hardly an option.

So in the last 20 years, we've made astronomical strides in terms of language learning. Immersion focused learning has generally been regarded, hands down, as the best and most effective way to learn a language. There are manifold reasons to this, but the biggest is that we are born to learn language.

Think about it like this: the Earth is absolutely *full* of creatures. Different species roam everywhere. The world is littered with different animals which took different evolutionary paths and yet humans are the only ones with language. Why is this?

Well, because if we didn't have it, then frankly we'd be at the bottom of the food chain. We diverged in such a way that we had to figure out how to work together towards common goals. We had to learn how to work together and communicate. So in a sense, your brain is not only *driven* to learn more languages. It's in fact explicitly *motivated* to learn language, whether it be early on in our lives or at a later point. We are *made* to learn and speak language. Saying anything else is terribly dishonest to ourselves.

The fastest way for us to learn languages is to immerse in it as much as possible, because such a method taps into those historic and prehistoric methods of language acquisition that we had to adapt to and still have to adapt today, if not even *more* so due to the fact that society has gotten so advanced to the point that we literally cannot live without learning another language.

Because immersion is such a great way to learn a language, language-learning methods which are *centered* around immersion have actually started popping up since the advent of the information age. An example of such is the extremely popular Benny Lewis's Fluent in 3 Months program; this Irish linguistic anomaly went from a person who only spoke English to somebody who now speaks seven languages fluently and four well. There are also numerous websites and applications which aim to teach one specifically how to use various languages, or vocabulary at the very least. As you very well may have guessed, we're going to be trying to implementing those into our language learning process to some extent in a manner which we'll discuss more later.

So what exactly is this book's approach? Well, you may have bought it alongside my others, or you may have bought it as a stand-alone book. Its first purpose is to accompany my other books I've written as a means of offering you a surefire way to become an absolutely fantastic speaker of any language. However, its secondary purpose is to outline a cohesive method of language learning that will really help you to get to the bulk of the language that you wish to learn and ascend to linguistic heights that you're only daydreaming of right now.

So in that pursuit, here are the things which this book is going to attempt to do.

First, you need to get into the mindset of language learning. So many people talk about how they can't do this or that. The rest of the book will be rather technical, but learning a language - as with learning anything else - requires a lot of dedication and, indeed, confidence in your ability to perform with it.

The second thing that we're going to talk about is analyzing the key concepts of a language, recognizing its differences from your own rather than its similarities, and then indeed learning and applying the essential concepts of the language.. If you've read or will read any of my other books, you'll notice that this is indeed a rather common motif that I express regularly. In my opinion, there is nothing more necessary and paramount when you're learning a new language than having a firm grasp on the grammatical concepts underlying said language. I'll discuss in greater detail why this is absolutely necessary in chapter two.

The third thing that we're going to cover is the absolutely critical importance of immersion and how to use it to your benefit in order to build your knowledge of the language as well as your vocabulary. I heavily disagree with the academic method of teaching vocabulary to wishful language students by heaping it on them and making them memorize it for an upcoming test and then hardly using it again if it's not related to the next pertinently covered topic. But that's a grievance for another day (or another chapter, at least.)

The fourth and final thing that we're going to cover and which makes up this method in an essential manner is the importance of *usage*. Usage is the point at which a lot of the previously talked about topics come together and usage is what is actually going to teach you to speak and communicate in the language. *Usage* in some contexts will also naturally build your vocabulary as well as reinforcing some bizarre concepts which may otherwise escape you, like the conjugation of irregular verbs.

So that makes up the four points of my language learning methodology: *study* the history, *break down* the language, *immerse* yourself, and *use* what you've learned. It's very bare-bones and my presentations of these given topics haven't been as great due to the brevity with which I'm presenting them, but you've got my solemn guarantee that everything will click for you as you read this book just as it did for me.

There are plenty of books on this subject on the market, thanks again for choosing this one! Every effort was made to ensure it is full of as much useful information as possible, please enjoy!

Chapter 1: Get into the Mindset

There are two different primary mindsets to language acquisition in the world right now. There are more in other subsets, but the two most commonly encountered are the academic sort - the sort which has you sitting in a classroom, possibly all day, drilling you with vocabulary lessons and grammatical concepts in an academic context - and the immersive sort - these are the ones which are generally espoused by polyglots, so I think that taking time in order to establish how you can work within this framework is super important.

I don't think there's anything explicitly wrong with the academic manner. But I do think it has its shortcomings as a form of language pedagogy intended for simple and natural language learning.

The reason that we use classrooms in order to teach things and we teach in such book-based ways in general is that teaching the myriad lessons which are taught at an institution like so demands that one have dedicated linear study. For a great many things, this works well. Mathematics, a musical instrument, chemistry, and so forth. For linguistics, it *can* work, but it's very far detached from our natural forms of language learning.

What actually works best for linguistics, many have found - it's not a universal thing, remember, but it's just the thing which works best for the majority of people - is an *immersion* based learning experience. Or in other words, an experience where they're surrounded by the language and are practicing it not just in the context of tests and flash cards, but in the television they watch, the applications on their phone, the people that they talk to, and so on.

I've spoken to a lot of people in my life who have tried to learn this or that language. They always tell me that "I'm just not cut out for learning languages" or something like that, and it's absurd.

I'm going to be honest: the traditional methods for language learning require a certain amount of passivity. We aren't made to learn language passively. It's not something that we're created to do. And when people are sitting in classrooms learning drab vocab which may or may not be something they'll actually talk about, I can't help feel like there's a lack of proper action or motivation. Often, too, that's what will kill the person's ability to learn: an utter lack of motivation due to the fact that they couldn't care less about the thing they're learning.

Let me make this clear: language learning is *not* easy. It can be made *easier*, but it's not *easy*. Saying that you expect to learn a language in a month or with only ten minutes of practice a day is a lot like those diet pills that proclaim themselves to be some kind of snake oil that will make you shed 100 pounds in a year: it doesn't happen. Full stop. It is *possible* to learn a language very quickly - in two to three months - with absolute dedication and what actually totals out to a lot of hard work, just like it's *possible* to lose 100 pounds in a year. However, it is not a passive activity.

Language learning happens in three ways:

1) Receiving input
2) Generating output
3) Receiving feedback/correction

It's through these three alone that you're going to learn a language. The input could be anything. It could be a gigantic "For Dummies" book that walks through every step of the language for beginners, or it could be a barebones explanatory sheet that teachers the person the basics before putting them on their own.

The output happens in one way only: you personally creating the phrases from the concepts that you know and from the things that you know. This is the only way that output can happen.

Receiving feedback and correction happens through somebody more proficient in the language than you are correcting you on this topic or that of the language after hearing you speak. They could be anybody from a teacher to a pen-pal to a girlfriend who was fluent in the language. It doesn't matter, what matters is that somehow and some way you're getting it.

So with those aspects of language learning fleshed out, now what we need to settle is how we can get those. The fact is that a lot of people, and in fact a lot of traditional language learning systems, will put up a fight against these natural language learning mechanisms. But I refuse to do that.

Here are the things that I'm going to emphasize from a standpoint of your demeanor towards language learning:

- *Passion* for the language
- *Connection* to the content
- *Immersion* rather than arbitrary rote memorization
- *Confidence* in your ability to speak
- *Willingness* to go out of your comfort zone.

You need a *passion* for the language if you want to learn it. Even a fake one, if you have to conjure one up out of thin air. At the beginning, learning a language is going to be awful. You're not going to know anything, you're going to be extremely lost and confused. You have to care enough about the language that you're working with that you can just keep on going with it even through rough patches and plateaus.

You need a *connection* to the content if you genuinely want to retain it. I find that in a lot of people, the only way for them to remember something is if they find that to some degree they care about it. This doubles up on the first point by reinforcing the idea that if you care about something, you're more likely to both work hard on it and to retain it.

You need *immersion* rather than rote memorization because immersion is going to teach you to use the language everywhere and use context to figure out new words and sounds. This is how we naturally learn our first languages and it's how we can naturally learn even more if we manage to tap into that primitive "lightbulb" notion of making things click and making gears simply turn. This builds upon the first and second points because I insist that you immerse yourself in topics that you care about, and help you to seek them out.

You need *confidence* in your ability to speak. Not in your ability to speak the *language*, you're going to be awful at the language for a long time. You need to accept that. "A long time" could be any number of measures from a month to several years. You have to realize that your reinforcement and your feedback is only going to come by speaking to people you've never spoken to before in a language that you're not entirely comfortable in. By getting out of that comfort zone and getting comfortable "being wrong", as well as by accepting that you will often flub up in seemingly simple ways, you will become a better speaker of the language even faster.

Lastly, you need *willingness* to go out of your comfort zone. This is something that only you can give yourself. I can harp on how important this and that thing is all that I want, but ultimately it's up to *you* to summon the willpower to actually make something happen for yourself in the context of language learning.

You'll need to summon a lot of willpower, in fact. This method is "fast and easy", but it's most certainly *not* a timesaver. If you want to learn a language in 10 minutes per day, you should relegate yourself to barely knowing the language in 4 years' time. If you want to learn it faster, you have to accept that your entire world will be in that language now, to the extent that you can make it so, and you have to accept that you're going to be spending an hour or two working in that language, translating both to and from, and that's not even including any time that you spend talking to your tutor.

But if you follow through with this method, I can guarantee you that you'll be a great speaker of whatever language it is that you want to speak.

Chapter 2: Break Down the Language

This is the single most important part of this entire book. Regardless of how you decide to learn after this - whether you decide to go an immersive route or a more traditional route - it will help you immensely in your journey if you break down the language that you're working with as well as language in a general sense so that you better understand exactly what you're working with.

I'd liken it somewhat to building a house on uneven land. You're going to need a *solid* foundation in place, regardless of whether the house that you build on it is in the Gothic style, the Colonial style, the Tudor style, or the Southwestern style.

The foundation of your language will be built in two parts: understanding the concepts of language *in general*, which I'm going to help you with in this chapter, as well as understanding the concepts of language *specific to your own*, which is something that's going to require some time spent in personal study and reflection on the language.

You also need this foundation in order to build whatever house you're trying to build. If you try to build a house without a foundation, it's going to fall apart. And that's truer than pretty much everything for this super immersion heavy manner of learning: if you don't set aside time in order to focus in and learn these basic building blocks of the language, you will not succeed, point blank. You will be weighed down by the intermediate difficulty of the sources you'll be surrounding yourself with and you'll fail to understand a lot of the nuance involved with the language.

See, the reason this works is because language serves a single purpose among people. It came about for one reason, and one reason solely: to communicate information. And because of this, it is very good at that specific purpose. And language offers many nuances between them all in order to discuss the caveats of a basic situation. You can take a basic phrase, sure, but you can also add a lot of detail. "The boy is tossing the ball" could become "The young boy is tossing a red ball to the dog while his mother sits on the porch and smiles."

What I'm saying is that all situations have a logical conclusion based off of the things which we can deduce about it with our own senses. As a result of this, we can surmise that all language is, indeed, intended to refer to the situations which arise around us. And indeed, language *does* serve this purpose. Because language has served a common purpose, the structures that have developed are similar as well. Our cognition reduces everything to a logical ultimate which is then expressed through words even in languages which are unrelated.

Believe it or not, most languages were once upon a time more related than they are today. Due to the patterns of conquest and migration patterns, language would actually develop both outward and inward and would change great volumes as time went on. There are a lot of reasons for this. The languages which preceded the great changes are commonly referred to as "proto-languages".

The vast majority of languages in Eurasia can be traced back to Proto-Indo-European, also called PIE. This language is by far the best understood proto-language. A huge number of languages in both Europe and Asia can be traced back to this lineage of languages. When you follow this lineage back and try to understand where and why each form departs, you're involved in what is actually a super interesting study; an inquiry into the origins and history of a great portion of language.

So because of this alone, a great number of the languages that you may desire to learn are related in some way or another, down the line. Their syntax, of course, has definitely changed in some capacity or another since those days long ago, but that's just the natural march of language. The point I'm trying to make here is that those languages have concepts in common.

And the languages which aren't related in such a manner to Proto-Indo-European will still share many of these same features, just because they're simply required in order to form a rational thought or delineate any sort of idea. So what this means is that even if you want to speak something like Mandarin Chinese or Lao or Hebrew or Arabic, they'll still share these key concepts because the singular purpose of language is to make logical inferences based off of events. At some point, every language evolved from a tribe of people needing to say things like "Let's settle here" - "You need to milk the cow" - "How can we best grow this plant?" - "There are migrating bison out to the west that we can kill." And indeed, the vast differences between multiple languages sets you up for a great number of uniformities among them.

So, this means that we can separate our language learning process into a lot of smaller and more malleable chunks that you can take advantage of and utilize one at a time in order to get a sound result.

Learn the Differences

This point can't be made enough. I've already made apparent that languages are contextually very similar. This means that if you spend a lot of time learning the similarities between a language, you're going to find a lot of them. A whole lot of them.

I know this is a really easy mistake to make, because when I first embarked on my language learning adventures, I started out by Googling "what language is the easiest for a person to learn?" My desire to be worldly and bilingual conflicted heavily with the amount of work I was truly willing to put out in return for such a thing. As I'm sure is no surprise, it didn't really work out for me.

What I should have done *instead* of learning what was within my comfort zone was ignore that another language would be out of my comfort zone entirely. There's no reason to think that, because every language will be out of your comfort zone. When you're learning another language, there is no such *thing* as a comfort zone, because every language will differ from your own (though possibly in varying degrees).

This is to say that when I say to learn the differences, I don't mean at the theoretical level; you're not at all ready for that sort of thing just yet. Instead, just do a cursory review of things such as the Wikipedia article for the language. When you do this, you'll be able to see not only the history of the language but also a few things about it. There are certain terms that will scare you or confuse you at first - for example, *agglutinative,* which means nothing linguistically to English speakers because English isn't agglutinative - but there will normally be at the very least a cursory explanation of the term within parentheses, or a link to the article on that concept itself which will normally provide both an in-depth examination and cumulative overview of the topic.

Why learn the differences before you get too into the language itself? Because that's how it works. You have to be prepared for whatever you may be facing. For example, if you were wanting to learn Chinese, it'd suit you well to know essential things which cause it to differ from English. For example, it's a tone language, as opposed to English which isn't. The meaning of words in Chinese can change drastically depending upon the tone in which you say the word. A person with bad tones in China sticks out like a sore thumb, though as a Westerner you'll probably get a pass for even trying to learn their language in the first place.

In other words, you've just got to know what to expect, or else you may find yourself completely blind-sided by a language in some ways or another. This is the last thing you want. You need to know what to expect going into the language so that you're actually prepared and not scrambling when some technique presents itself.

Now with that little aspect out of it all, it's time to move onto the technical aspects: the things you need to learn before doing anything else.

Learn the Alphabet

This seems a little terse, I'm sure. But the fact is that there are a lot of languages which don't have Latin alphabets or even anything close. Let me put it this way: there are a lot of languages which you don't understand, and there are a lot of alphabets, too, that you don't understand.

I can think of several off of the top of my head.

First, there's *Cyrillic script*, which is used heavily by Russia, though also by countries which have developed in its approximate proximity. Languages which use the Cyrillic script include but are certainly not limited to Russian, Ukrainian, Mongolian, Kazakh, and Macedonian.

Then there are the Semitic scripts like Arabic and Hebrew. You need to learn these before doing anything else, however you can. This is for the simple fact that they can be convoluted and confusing, but also because a nifty feature of these scripts is that they can completely exclude vowels and leave you to just decipher a word based upon context. This is actually a really cool linguistic model based upon triconsonantal roots, but it can be very confusing as a beginner. It becomes even more confusing when you're trying to struggle with the basic alphabet on top of that. The alphabet should without a doubt be the first thing that you learn in these languages.

Then, for example, there's the Korean script *hangul*. This is a really simple script to learn and understand, especially because it was created specifically for Korean by a single guy in order to make Korean far easier to read. However, the case here is much like a less serious version of the case for semitic scripts: the vast majority of the source material that you'll be encountering and even language-teaching guides you may encounter will invariably be written to some extent in the language itself.

This method has some shortcomings, overall. I'll admit that. It doesn't work well for logographic languages. Logographic languages are languages which, as opposed to an alphabet crafted from individual graphs which all represent a singular sound consistently, have instead a unique character for every single word in the language. A beautiful example of a logographic language is Chinese, and Japanese would be another sterling example as well (aside from Katakana). For logographic languages, the only way at all to really learn the language is to practice it. The only way around this is if you decide to learn how things sound when they're Romanized and learn the Romanized version of the language at a faster rate than you're learning the logographic characters. You can base the characters that you're learning off of the words that you already know. This is the only feasible way I can imagine taking my language learning method and applying it to logographic languages, and it's possible but will certainly be difficult due to the lack of a real wealth of Romanized resources in these languages available for you to learn by.

Learn the Structure

Once you know the alphabet, you need to learn about the structure of a language. Languages are essentially composed of three different extremely basic components: subjects, objects, and verbs. There isn't a language that lacks any of these three components. I'll explain them more in a second.

English, for reference, is a subject-verb-object language. This is massively different compared to, say, Japanese, which is a subject object verb language, or

Arabic, which is a verb subject object language.

So what does this mean exactly? This refers to the order of the given parts of speech in a conventional sentence within the language.

Subjects - Subjects are the things which the sentence is based around. However, since this can be a little vague, it's better defined as the thing which ultimately controls or is the progenitor of the verb. The reason I add the progenitor clause is because in the sentence "It is nice," the subject is still *it* because the verb *is* (a conjugated form of *to be*) has to do directly with the verb *it*. *It* is existing in such a manner, so it's acceptable to say "It is", even if "it" isn't doing anything directly with the verb "is". Subjects are also called the *nominative case* should you be working with a language which has a form or noun declension.

Verbs - Verbs are the actions which are undertaken, but they can also indicate things such as an occurrence of some sort (*to become*) or a given state (*to exist*). Verbs usually are conjugated in a certain way to their speaker, though they aren't conjugated in every language. It will vary depending mostly upon which language exactly you're speaking. But a huge number of languages have this feature, called both verb inflection and verb conjugation. All that it means is that they are changed in a certain way to agree with any number of characteristics of either the subject or the object (generally the subject), such as gender, plurality, and perspective (first person, second person, third person). Languages which are based around this concept will generally require a lot of work to understand how verbs work and how you can make them come naturally. Languages which don't have this concept make up for the difficulty elsewhere. There are actually a lot more things to verbs, such as intransitive verbs vs. transitive verbs (which pertains to whether or not they utilize a direct object), linking verbs, and so on. It really depends upon the language that you're specifically studying as to how it implements it.

Objects - Objects are the things which are on the other side of the verb. This may sound obvious and vague, but the truth is that defining objects can be a little tricky. The general definition is usually something along the lines of "the word which is affected by the verb." This can be a little tricky, however. Objects are generally divided into two classes: direct objects and indirect objects. I make this distinction in every language book I write and am certain to make the lines between them very clear. There are a lot of ways to divide and define the two, but the way that I find most useful to describe the difference between the two is by making a very clear delineation between the required nature of the two. This is to say that if you have a direct object, you can't remove it from the sentence and have it makes sense, whereas indirect objects serve a purely contextual purpose. Consider the sentence "He writes the book with me." We can divide this into its parts: "He *mails* **the book** <u>with me</u>." In this case, the subject is left unstylized, the verb is italicized, the direct object is emboldened, and the indirect object is underlined. You can see easier now the relationship between the verb and the direct object. If you were to say "He mails with me.", it would make absolutely no sense at all. People would be wondering "he mails *what* with me?" The direct object is what answers that question of *what* in sentences. However, if we were to take out the indirect object instead, like so: "He mails the book", it would make perfect sense. Indirect objects most of the time do little more than provide context. The phrase "He says it to me." is similar: the *to me*, while essential to the point of the sentence, is purely contextual and the sentence would be grammatically sound without that.

Anyhow, those are the three main components of a sentence across languages. It would serve you well to understand them all to the maximum capacity you can within your own language. Does the subject come before the verb? After? Where does the object go? Not every sentence in every language works like English sentences do. You have to remember that language has as much, if not more, societal deviation than separate cultures. The conditions which created any two given languages are never the same, and so they'll have grown differently and may have even had a completely different basis. For an example of this sort of growth, *PIE* was originally a subject object verb sentence, as were Ancient Greek and Latin. However, as they would grow and develop, they would change this order entirely. And it's not unusual for this sort of thing to happen over periods of vast linguistic growth. English, for example, dropped the idea of verb-second word order altogether.

As you read through all of this, you should be simultaneously learning *how*. This is how you're going to build your foundation: learning exactly how all of it works. You aren't going to go very far if you don't take the time to do all of this.

For subjects, it's imperative that you learn every possible subject pronoun and, a little later, every possible object pronoun. You're going to be using these and seeing these extensively for the simple reason that they're everywhere. There isn't a sentence which can work without a subject. Well, there are, but they aren't valid sentences generally. There are some sentences, such as Spanish, which allow you to drop the subject due to the conjugation, but this is for the simple reason that the subject is implied through the conjugation of the sentence. Conversely, French doesn't work in such a manner; you *have* to either say a subject pronoun or you have to mention a specific subject alongside a very specific article which denotes exactly what you're talking about. This is because all of the first-person verbs mesh together on their endings and you can only tell them apart if there's liaison involved, often. So regardless of what the specific system for subjects is within the language that you're going to be working with, it's your job to understand them to the best extent which you can.

Now, speaking in terms of verbs, I've mentioned before my disdain for classroom style vocabulary learning, and going along with that, I don't think the best way to learn verbs is in that manner. However, and that's a big however, you do need to recognize verb inflection if there is such a thing, or any other manners of recognizing verbs so that you can actually work with and understand them, as well as recognize them when they show up in the text. Additionally, you really need to learn the basic verbs, and unfortunately, there will often be a lot of irregular verbs that are completely detached from any notion of normal conjugation or declension. Even in Chinese, which has *no* verb conjugation system, there are two verbs which have a marker afterwards that is irregular. These form naturally, honestly, after a long period of language speaking. This is exacerbated by the general lack of print or text reproduction technology for most of history. Alongside the general lack of literacy came a lack of standardization, which made it rather difficult to have any sort of uniformity among the language as it would grow and develop. So the changes which would occur were very massive and sweeping, and also led to some verbs losing any sort of standardized form. Perhaps such is a bit natural after several millennia of linguistic divergence, but I digress. You're going to have to practice 1) recognizing verb inflections for regular verbs, and recognizing those verbs when they pop up in the text and 2) at the *least*, the ten most common irregular verbs for the language that you're learning (if it should have that many; some don't.)

The only other trouble you'll run into in the sphere of verbs if you do those two things is understanding idiomatic expressions, or phrases which don't mean expressly what they say they mean. An example of an idiom in English would be "it's raining cats and dogs". It's not *literally* raining cats and dogs, but it is raining quite hard if one says such a thing. With that said, though, if you follow the language acquisition tips that I outline in the chapter after this one, you should these idioms through your personal translation efforts.

When it comes to verb tenses, you don't have to know every single tense. It's worthwhile for you to learn the most common past tense and future tense if they exist, though. For example, in French, this would be the passé composé and either the simple future or the *futur proche,* meaning "close future". I use French as an example because it's the language I know best, but this applies to any given language. Some languages don't have a "past tense" verb conjugation per se and have a different way of showing past tense. Either way, you're going to need to know how to use that part of speech, as well as understand how it will show up in both speech and text.

The last thing is the object. Objects generally aren't too terribly difficult to learn across languages and are typically actually one of the easier things of understand because most of the time, they'll be composed of either a noun, an article and a noun, or a preposition and a noun. The hard part is more understanding the articles and prepositions of the language so that you can recognize the indirect objects when you see them. Some languages do bizarre things with objects, but by studying the broad concept of objects within the language, then you'll be able to start to understand.

I just mentioned articles and prepositions. I do think it's absolutely necessary that you understand articles before you go any further with your language learning. This won't apply to every language - some languages don't have what we'd commonly refer to as articles, or they have them in a far different way than we'd recognize. However, it's still worth researching and finding your answer so that you can learn as to whether the given language does have them or not. Articles are things which specify the *number* and *location* of a given noun. For example, if I were to say "I ate *a* slice of pizza", it would indicate that that I ate some non-specific piece of pizza. This is commonly referred to as an indefinite article. If I were to say "I ate *the* slice of pizza", it's implied that I'm referring to a very explicit slice of pizza, not just any slice off of the street. Maybe somebody asked me what happened to a very specific slice of pizza, and I responded in accordance. This is called a *definite* article. There are also other types of articles. "This" and "that" could be considered articles - "I ate *this* slice of pizza" refers to a specific slice which you are demonstrating, where "I ate *that* slice of pizza" means you're referring to a specific slice which is elsewhere from you. The simple correlation for this is usually "this" -> "here", "that" -> "there". Articles are essential because, especially with languages like Danish and Swedish, if you don't know them, they will almost certainly get lost in the text. It's not that they're hard to understand, but it's that if you *don't* understand them, you're at a massive disadvantage.

On a related note to articles and prepositions, you may run across the notion of "gendered" nouns. This doesn't refer to a physical characteristic so much as a linguistic development. Nouns, especially in Romance languages, which have genders have such because it produces vowel harmony, and they just happen to sound best with the articles and pronouns which would be used to reference male and female human beings. Some languages will also have a *neuter* gender which will make it an even more confusing mess. But really, it doesn't quite matter on the origin of these, what matters more is that you learn the nuances of noun gender for your particular language if such a thing exists for it.

Anyhow, the next thing that you're going to want to learn is prepositions. It's important to learn at least the most basic of prepositions, because prepositions are what allow you to express yourself on a higher level. Prepositions open the door for not only idiom but for phrases which allow you to imply or explicitly state an object's location. Prepositions in English were always explained to me in grade school as "places where a squirrel can go": a squirrel can go in, out, around, through, and so forth... it wasn't a perfect explanation and it certainly is lacking in the proper nuance, but it does fit the bill pretty well. Some prepositions are absolutely essential, such as *à* in French: it's used for both location as well as a helping article in transitive verbs and general things of that nature. You have to seriously take time to learn at least the most basic of prepositions in whatever language that you're trying to learn so that you can better know what you're working with as you go forward.

What's more is that you need to learn basic conversational phrases. This is because these vary from language to language and it can be a little bizarre trying to translate some of them directly because a lot of them have no direct translation. Some of them have been the same for centuries while other aspects of the language have changed, which can make it a really bizarre experience. So the best thing to do, really, is to learn them as their own unit. Learn things like "hello", "goodbye", "thank you", and "please", alongside how to get to a certain place and how to ask for help. The other plus side is that since you've already looked a great deal into the formation of verbs and subjects and objects, you'll be able to pick each out of the sentence and likely increase your vocabulary to a certain extent.

    The last thing that you really need to focus on picking up in terms of background knowledge is learning how to ask *questions* in the given language. This, too, will vary from language to language, and rather greatly at that. But asking questions is a major part of any conducive conversation. On top of that, you're going to have to work with questions in order to ask people how to get around or for the help that you'll inevitably need.

    After you've built a solid foundation and you feel like you know the most essential parts of the language well, even if your vocabulary isn't excellent, then you're ready to move forward into the immersive part of this method.

Chapter 3: Immerse Yourself

A few years ago, I tried to learn Latin from a book. It was a rather archaic book written by a well-meaning professor sometime in the 1970s or 1980s; well, I say that, but the reality is that it was written a bit later, likely in the mid-1990s, its methodology just *seemed* so outdated. This is when I began to realize a lot of the structural problems of language learning and why people become so disenfranchised with it so fast.

We already talked in chapter one about how people tend to give up learning a language because it's just "simply not for them." When they say this, I sigh, and not for them and not out of pity, but rather out of regret that we've managed to build a manner of educating people on languages that manages not to *teach* a many people who fall into these language learning classes, but rather to have them *pass a test*.

It's my firm belief, as I've already said, that not only are people *able* to learn, but they're *made* to learn language. However, just as we tend to take the fun out of a great many things in academia, language learning itself has been relegated to being a book-y study-wrought subject rather than what it actually is: an opportunity to meet new souls that you've never met before, to talk to and intertwine with people that you normally never would have because you don't even speak the same language.

See, language learning is actually a beautiful experience. By learning a language, you're allowing yourself to see into a whole new world of culture and alternative thought. Some places are a bigger departure from your customs than others, but every single place has its own unique story. What's neat is that language not only allows you to *experience* this story, but you also get to *get* some of this story from the language itself. My favorite example of this is Spanish. Spanish is a language of a territory in heavy dispute and intrinsic conflict for centuries. In their language, you find the culture of a great numerous conquests against the Spanish, most notably by the Arabs who had taken control of Spain for some 3 or 4 centuries in the first and second millennium. This is evident in the fact that Spanish had actually adopted a huge number of words from those who had conquered them - Arabic words which would come to represent either new concepts in Spain or replace the go-to word for old concepts. Of course, these weren't entirely pervasive, but their presence is noteworthy nonetheless. If you were to open a Spanish dictionary and flip back to the opening pages, you'd see several pages of words which begin with "al", which means they were more than likely taken from Arabic, which had an article "*al*" meaning "*the*".

So how we manage to turn that into a dull classroom experience is *beyond* me. Language learning itself is little more than a door to a whole new world of experiences. Sure, the lock may be a bit difficult to figure out, exactly, but the contents on the other side of the door make it worth it.

That's beside the point, though: language is an *intrinsically social* concept. It would make absolutely zero sense if you learned a new language to talk about something that you don't care about. So why would you try to go forward with learning a language if it meant doing so in a manner which you don't care about and frankly couldn't really care *less* about? It's an absolute recipe for disaster.

What I propose to you instead is a method I've developed during my language studies which I refer to as *usage-based vocabulary learning*. There's actually another method and component to this whole lesson: *passion-based immersion*.

Let me break this down.

The idea behind this theory is rather simple: we learn best when we're actually using things that we learn. Likewise, for the vast majority of people who would be categorized as kinetic learners, they learn by active usage and reinforcement of concepts and scouring out solutions if they can't find them in the first place.

What I've developed is a far more hands-on method to vocabulary increasing than what the norm is. Note that I'm not completely disowning the concept of traditional vocabulary learning, and it can, in fact, be beneficial. Rather, what I'm decrying is the idea of using *solely* traditional vocabulary learning and taking in heaps of words and then never using them again until a long time down the road.

My train of thought in developing this was actually based off of an experience I had a while back when I was learning French, my first secondary language. I had been trodding along for a while but hardly making genuine progress. I had taken it all throughout high school and would occasionally dabble with it but didn't make a lot of sense of it. It sounds really small, but at one point I discovered that the United Kingdom equivalent to the United States word "eggplant" was "aubergine", which reminded me of the French term I'd remembered some years ago but long forgotten, or at least certainly wouldn't have been able to recall. I suppose the association between the English and the French term jarred my recollection. But at that point, I started thinking about how I remembered that word solely by making a connection, and I realized that past a certain point, the totality of language learning is the gentle art of making things click.

It seems like a rather small incident and it was, for certain - but the consequences of it, the train of thought which resulted, made me get back to learning French by way of *practicing* it. If I ever needed a word, the beauty of the information age meant that I could just go to a website and find a nearly direct translation, along with a sentence and comparative context. That was a huge boon to my ability to speak French well and I realized that I was growing quickly and had made on my own a realization that every great language learner has made: language learning, whether it be your first language or your fifth language, always occurs because you see/hear a word you don't know, analyze the context, and give that word a context. So if it works that way, I reasoned, why couldn't the opposite be true? Why couldn't we have a *context* that we didn't know how to explain, and learn the language through adjustment and effort to those given contexts? The same mechanism of making things "click" is present within both actions, so long as you know the basics of the language that the words you're presenting for your context aren't either outlandishly difficult or impossible to parse given your understanding of a language.

Anyway, having made this realization and being the aspiring poet that I was at that point, I took to writing quite a bit of poetry. This helped me greatly in learning the uses of various words I *did* know as I would research them for correctness, as well as allowing me to practice them, and it also helped me to increase my vocabulary because I had specific ideas that I was trying to convey.

That's why one of the pillars which I recommend to you as a language learner is the following: find a way to **use** your language. There is absolutely no way around this step. As a new speaker, you may feel a tad uncomfortable using it around other people, and that's okay (even though you'll have to sometime.) What I recommend that you do instead is start writing a nightly journal, recounting your day in the language which you were trying to learn, and expressing any thoughts you might have otherwise in the language as well. Do this daily, regardless of whether you're talking to people in the given language yet or not. There is no way around this task. It's simple, it doesn't take terribly long, and it's the most effective form of study that you can undertake: that which allows you to truly *express*.

There are a great number of reasons that you should take my advice and write a nightly journal in the language of your choosing. The first, of course, is that it allows you to practice the language. The second is that you're going to naturally pick up a lot more words. You'll get a lot of experience using common expressions and you'll find yourself feeling like more of a natural when it comes to things like irregular verbs or noun declension. Even things like verb conjugation will come out to be much easier for you. Write your *thoughts*, studiously, and if you ever have a question about whether a certain verb tense exists in the language you're studying, or whether a certain word exists, then I implore you to *research it*.

The truth is that you have *got* to learn vocabulary somehow. There are a lot of ways to do it. But when it comes between a method which works on our intuitive capacity to learn and utilize language, and one which just requires rote memorization of given concepts which we may or may not use at a later point, I will always opt for the first.

This is the first time that I've published this method, so my sample size is rather small; in fact, it consists solely of myself. But I genuinely believe that this specific method of acquiring new vocabulary in a language is far better than the traditional method.

As I said though, there's still a lot of room for traditional vocabulary learning in the sense of non-usage memorization techniques. In fact, as a standalone tactic, there's nothing intrinsically *wrong* with them as a primary language learning route. It's just that there's an option which is *better* as a primary language learning route, because it actively engages you. I genuinely believe that to some degree we've surpassed the archaic notions of rote memorization, because when I hear that I can't help recalling about the tutored children in Greece who were required to recite epic poems.

With that said, there is certainly and without a doubt a place for them as a *secondary* method of language acquisition, and I do certainly encourage you to use them in this manner. I believe that the most well-known example of these rote-memorization services being used as a sort of way to reinforce grammar and explore vocabulary is the *Duolingo* service available at (http://duolingo.com), though if you're learning Chinese you may be inclined to look at "Hello Chinese" (http://hellochinese.cc) which is very similar to China.

I think that grammar and vocabulary are two distinct phenomena, in a way. I think that grammar requires independent case-related study - you aren't going to remember how to form, for example, the imperfect tense in Italian if you aren't actively using it in any way - so you should research it as you need it in your personal writings and so that you're prepared to use it *next* time you need to. Basically everything about this language acquisition method is diametrically opposed to anything that requires you to memorize something *before* you run across it naturally.

In other words, I don't feel like there's anything very organic about learning a language by remembering words on a page. And likewise, I think that since it's such an inorganic method of language acquisition, I don't think that people who decide to use this specific route of language acquisition are going to go terribly far at all with it.

I know what you're thinking: "If I wait to learn these things until I need them, then how am I going to know how to use them when I need them?"

I understand that concern entirely. I will say that your basic introductions to a language should always include how to form the past tense or, in the few languages for which there isn't a specific past tense, how to indicate something happened in the past, just in case you run into a need for it. However, here are two facts:

1) When I say you need to learn things as you encounter a need to learn

them, I don't mean that every time you need a word should be when you're out in the streets needing help for this or that. What I mean is that you need to practice a direct yet detached method of language acquisition which focuses on the *organic* process of interpreting and understanding new terms as opposed to the process which focuses entirely on the sole acquisition of new terms that many language learning courses devolve into.
2) Kindness is a human trait. No matter how much people tell you otherwise, for the vast majority of people, the default will always be kindness. So if you walk into a place in a foreign country and have to fumble with the language, they won't be angry and they won't be upset with you. Learning somebody else's language is a show of *respect*, not disrespect, and they will only respect you and try to help you for learning their culture. Most people are proud of where they come from to some extent or another, and anything respect paid to the culture of where they call "home" is looked kindly upon. So there's nothing wrong with speaking a Pidgin version of a language or hardly knowing how to conjugate verbs (though this isn't realistic if you're working with the language on a nightly basis).

The reason I say all of this is to articulate why I don't think that programs like Duolingo are great if they're the *only* source that you're working with. I just feel as though they fail in an essential way. If you are working with two concepts which beg development on their own accord, then the experience of learning both is diluted.

So I'm sure at this point you're skeptical. This is a little bit of a bizarre way to learn a language, I understand. But try it and you'll understand.

Let me now move onto the other part, which will hopefully clear up any residual concerns you have about the language learning process I'm suggesting, and the reason this chapter is called "Immerse yourself".

There are two sides to immersion: *ingoing* and *outgoing*. *Outgoing* is what we just talked about: the actual private usage of the language in order to develop your ability to speak in it. This is one essential part of this paradigm of language acquisition.

The other part then is obviously *incoming immersion*. These are the influences in the language that you're taking in from the *outside*. Language learning ideally should include a beneficial balance of both of these. I frankly have yet to figure out exactly what this balance should be, though.

So what, in my eyes, makes up *incoming immersion*? Anything that you experience in the language that allows you to make sense of something. These are things which act on those "make it click" mechanisms in our brains in order to connect certain lines between words and meaning in the new language. There are a lot of ways that you can actually achieve this.

The first is rather obvious: change the language of your phone and computer to the language you're wishing to learn. This specific suggestion may work better for languages in the Indo-European language family as it's much easier to "extrapolate" the meanings of vague phrases when they have a similar formation. This is pertinent when it comes to technology because certain things *are* in longer, complete sentences, but a huge number of things are not, like application names or menus in the Windows file explorer such as "This Computer". This isn't exclusively true, however, and if you have a knowledge of how the language is written, pronounced, and structured, it's probably in your best interest to immerse yourself in that manner.

The second is obvious as well: use subtitles to your advantage. Netflix has thousands of titles streaming that are available in multiple languages, as well as a huge number of films which are available in both English and alternative language subtitles as well. This can be extremely conducive to those "make it click" mechanisms because you're actively enthralled by the thing that you're watching.

My recommendation, should you decide to go along with this, is to start with English audio and subtitles in your given language *first*. After you're comfortable with the language, I would then switch over to the audio in your given language and English subtitles. The reason for this is that it's really easy to be confused or thrown off by a language's accent at first as a language learner, and I don't think that it's ultimately very conducive to try to wean words apart in the native language and give them an English meaning from the English subtitles if you don't know very much about the language. That sort of thing is more for learning supplementary words and idioms once you have a firm enough grasp of the language in other contexts. As you're starting out, you 110% should start with English audio, just because it allows you to get used to reading the given language and acquainting the many words you don't know at that point to their English equivalent rather than the converse. The power of audio only goes so far, and in English, you already know where words start and end. As a beginner in a new language, you often don't have such a privilege.

So as we go forward with the idea of ingoing immersion, we're coming to the topic that I mentioned earlier and that I think is ultimately one of the two most important things to take away from this chapter: *passion-based immersion*.

So what do I mean by this? It probably sounds a tad pretentious, I'm aware, but the meaning is pure.

Human interests arise as forces in society as people group together in order to talk about them and join in solidarity over their admiration for the given topic. That is to say that often these topics will cross the general lines of linguistic division and carry over across languages.

What's more is that we always learn better when it's something that we care about, or connected in a way, even only tangentially, to something that we care about. We're more likely to forge mental connections and remember things which need to be remembered if they're connected to something that we ultimately care about rather than something that we, well, don't.

This theory builds upon that idea. The premise is simple: take the things you like and take advantage of that in order to learn a new language. But the manifestation can be a tad difficult.

The exact advice for carrying this out really depends ultimately upon what your passions even *are*. Regardless of what they are, the chances are much better than the converse that the region where the language you're learning is either spoken currently or has had a presence before will have *some* sort of connection to the topic.

For example, let's take World War II. A lot of people are *greatly* interested in World War II as a general topic. By learning French or Russian, you could read about the events from either a French or a Soviet perspective respectively.

I guess the point I'm trying to make in this instance is that earlier, I mentioned that learning a language opens the door to a lot of culture. Well, by this point I've already enumerated many times over how important being passionate is to the idea of language learning and how much it will help you.

So what I'm telling you to do here is to connect those two ideals of regional culture and passion in some manner so that you can find a book written in the source language that you'll actually *want* to read. Every night, translate either a page or a paragraph depending upon both how big the book is and how much time you have to dedicate to this. At first, you're going to be fumbling around a lot and encountering a lot of words you don't know - that's absolutely fine and frankly it's to be very expected. However, you should after a while make your way to the end of the book, at which point you can get another book related to your passions and repeat the process.

There are a lot of resources for translation, but I absolutely can't get enough of WordReference (http://wordreference.com). They have extensive dictionaries for a great number of languages and, on top of that, they have a wonderful system for searching up not only words but also idioms, expressions, and common phrases.

After a while, you should make your way through the book and reread it. Translate again any words that you don't understand entirely, but this time around they should be much fewer.

This will inevitably be time-consuming, but learning a language works on an inverse relationship of *effort* and *time*: the more *effort* and study that you expend towards learning a language, the less overall *time* it will take you to learn a language. So what benefits does this serve, exactly? Many!

- This method allows you to work with something that you care about. As I've already said, this makes you much more likely to internalize the information than doing it in an alternative manner.
- Working with a new language constantly will allow you to become much stronger with it.
- There's a fixed motive of finish a page/paragraph which makes it easier to go through with, but not quite laborious since you care about the topic at hand.

I think the biggest thing which makes it a great asset is the fact that you *are* mentally connected to the topic after all, though. That means that it's going to be much easier for you to absorb the words that you translate.

I don't think you need to drill yourself learning vocabulary as you're starting out, though. I think you need to focus more on patterns. Every language has patterns. For example, adverbs in English end in *-ly*; in Spanish, they end in *-mente*; in French, they end in *-ment*, and so on. So many people become disenfranchised with learning languages because it just becomes a game of constant memorization. They'll be so disheartened and stressed out by having to memorize *x* set of words, and that stress actually makes it far harder to learn.

This is where I should give yet another disclaimer: I don't think that flashcard learning methods are explicitly bad, or any other popular method of vocabulary learning. I think it can be useful if you take the right mindset about it. However, once more, I don't think it should be your primary learning vehicle. Your primary learning vehicle should be *personal experience*, no questions asked. There's nothing that will benefit you so much as immersing yourself in something that you care about.

Chapter 4: Usage

So, we're nearing the end of the book and one thing has become incredibly apparent: none of this work that you've done matters if you aren't going to find a way to use the language and reinforce the things which you've already learned.

I mean sure, reading and writing will get you to a certain extent, but what really helps a person understand a language is, frankly, *using* it. Not in journals, not in just watching the television with subtitles or dubbed audio, but with actually using the language that you've developed it.

Thanks to the things we worked on in the first chapter, I dearly hope that you're at a point where you feel confident with not only what you do know but what you *don't* know, as well as with your ability to transfer both to the real world.

The simple fact is that as you speak to other people, you are going to make mistakes, and you are going to make quite a few. But it's really not so bad; we make mistakes in our *native* language all the time, yet nobody is embarrassed about them. Think about all the people who get extremely confused on the usage differences of "your" and "you're", or of "to" and "too" and "two". People tend not to notice these -- in fact, they proclaim them proudly by virtue of not noticing them.

But the thing is that you've got to do whatever you can to get out of your comfort zone and start speaking another language. You have to actually *use* the language. Strike up conversations with new people who speak the language. If you are studying at home, not abroad, then it may benefit you to find a pen-pal or a Skype partner. There are lots of these in lots of places, I recommend http://language-exchanges.org in order to find people that you can converse in your new language on Skype with. However, you can also go to http://italki.com, which is a paid service but very popular thanks to certain personalities promoting it.

Another thing that you can do is head to http://meetup.com. This is a beautiful resource for meeting other people who practice the same language that you do, and generally has people who are at multiple skill levels, from beginner to intermediate to expert to fluent. All that you do is go to the site and type in your location and type in the language as the keyword. Then search. I was able to find local groups with ease. If you live anywhere near a city, as most people do, you should be able to find some group which is somewhat relevant to your interests.

The purpose in all of these things I'm suggesting is to give you the chance to practice talking under pressure, as well as to meet new people. When you meet new people who speak a different language, you can subconsciously forge a barrier with them. It's somewhat like a mask at a masquerade; you can see behind it, but why would you want to? When you meet someone under the pretense of speaking another language, you speak to them *in that language*. You can work off of each other to develop if you're at about the same level and if they're at a better level (I advise making friends with at least one person who is at a better level linguistically than you are) then you can very easily be corrected instantaneously and try to have genuine conversations with real people.

The thing too is that when you meet people in this manner, you're still meeting *people*. People with childhoods, stories, alma maters and degrees, pets and children, girlfriends and boyfriends, people who have traveled, people who were raised in a different culture, and so on and so forth. The chances are very great that if you meet a person through this method, you're going to actually *want* to talk to them in the language, which will even further drive your desire to learn the language and speak it very well.

This is one of the shortest chapters in the book, I know, but its importance can't be understated. You're doing yourself a major disservice if you opt to not try to meet others who speak the language. It's only through positive real life reinforcement that you're going to develop into a master of whatever language it is that you've decided to practice.

Conclusion

Thank for making it through to the end of *Learn Languages: The fastest and easiest way to learn any foreign language*, let's hope it was informative and able to provide you with all of the tools you need to achieve your goals whatever it may be.

The next step is to take these things we've talked about and apply them. I've made it more than abundantly clear just how you can do that. You need to be the one to go outside of your comfort zone. Use words you don't quite understand, conjugate verbs in conversation that you're not quite familiar with, do anything and everything. It is only through use and reinforcement that you'll learn a language in a short amount of time.

I genuinely hope that the help I've tried to provide throughout the course of this book is something that you've found useful. It's my sincere goal as somebody who cares very genuinely about linguistics that you may use these tips in order to become a better speaker of another language, and that you may also be exposed to the concepts which I care so dearly about.

Finally, if you found this book useful in any way, a review on Amazon is always appreciated!

www.ingramcontent.com/pod-product-compliance
Lightning Source LLC
Chambersburg PA
CBHW081412070526
44583CB00020B/2778